40 Days to Stre~~ngthening Family~~

Day 1: The Foundation of a Str~~ong Family~~
Day 2: Cultivating Open Comm~~unication~~
Day 3: Making Quality Time a P~~riority~~
Day 4: Fostering Forgiveness and Reconciliation
Day 5: Strengthening Family Through Prayer
Day 6: Building a Supportive Home Environment
Day 7: The Importance of Family Traditions
Day 8: Developing Healthy Boundaries
Day 9: The Power of Parental Leadership
Day 10: Sibling Bonds and Relationships
Day 11: Encouraging Emotional Intelligence
Day 12: Nurturing Spiritual Growth in Children
Day 13: Overcoming Challenges as a Family
Day 14: The Value of Family Rituals
Day 15: Building Trust and Reliability
Day 16: Cultivating Empathy and Compassion
Day 17: Establishing Family Goals and Values
Day 18: Balancing Family, Work, and Leisure
Day 19: Creating a Culture of Service
Day 20: The Role of Faith in Family Life
Day 21: Resolving Conflicts with Love and Respect
Day 22: Learning to Listen and Understand
Day 23: Celebrating Individuality and Uniqueness
Day 24: The Power of Unconditional Love
Day 25: Fostering a Spirit of Gratitude
Day 26: Teaching Responsibility and Accountability
Day 27: Growing Together through Life Transitions
Day 28: Strengthening Family Bonds through Humor
Day 29: The Importance of Family Support Networks
Day 30: Encouraging Openness and Honesty
Day 31: The Role of Discipline in Family Life
Day 32: The Power of Family Prayer and Worship
Day 33: Developing Resilience as a Family
Day 34: Cultivating a Heart of Generosity
Day 35: Strengthening Marriage and Partnership
Day 36: Guiding Children through Spiritual Formation
Day 37: Embracing the Legacy of Family
Day 38: Building a Stronger Connection with Extended Family
Day 39: The Impact of Family on Personal Growth
Day 40: Celebrating the Journey of Family Life

Strengthening Family Bonds

There are few aspects of life that are as precious as the bonds we share with our families. However, in our increasingly busy and fast-paced world, it can be all too easy to neglect the nurturing and strengthening of these relationships.

This 40-day spiritual journey is designed to guide you and your loved ones through a transformative process of growth, reflection, and renewal, ultimately leading to deeper connections, improved communication, and greater love and unity within your family.

The family unit is a sacred and vital part of our lives, serving as a cornerstone for our emotional, physical, and spiritual well-being.

Our relationships with our spouses, children, siblings, and parents provide us with a sense of belonging, support, and love that can sustain us through life's challenges and hardships.

Moreover, our families are the first environments in which we learn about love, trust, and faith, shaping our characters and our relationships with others.

Throughout this journey, we will delve into the essential aspects of family life, focusing on principles that are rooted in faith and spirituality.

Each day, you will be provided with a thought-provoking scripture, an insightful reflection, and a prayer or meditation to guide your thoughts and actions, helping you to develop a deeper understanding of the role that faith plays in cultivating a strong and loving family.

As you embark on this journey, you may find that some days are more challenging than others, and that's okay.

Remember, the purpose of this journey is to foster growth and transformation, which is rarely a linear process.

Give yourself and your family members grace and patience as you navigate this journey together. Be open to the lessons that each day brings, and be willing to share your experiences and insights with one another.

Over the course of these 40 days, you will explore a wide range of topics, from establishing open communication and setting healthy boundaries to fostering forgiveness, encouraging spiritual growth, and nurturing the unique gifts and talents of each family member.

By committing to this journey and embracing the principles presented, you will be taking a powerful step towards strengthening the bonds of love and unity within your family.

This spiritual journey is meant to be an enriching and rewarding experience, one that brings you closer to your loved ones while deepening your connection with the divine.

As you progress through these 40 days, may you and your family be blessed with increased love, understanding, and unity, and may the transformative power of faith guide you along the path to a stronger, healthier, and more fulfilling family life.

Welcome to your 40 Days to Strengthening Family Bonds: A Spiritual Journey to Nurturing Love and Unity.

Let this journey begin.

Day 1: The Foundation of a Strong Family

Scripture:

"Unless the LORD builds the house, those who build it labor in vain. Unless the LORD watches over the city, the watchman stays awake in vain." - Psalm 127:1 (ESV)

Reflection:

A strong family is built upon a foundation that acknowledges the importance of spiritual values and principles. Recognizing the role of God in our lives and inviting Him into our families can help us create a more loving, nurturing, and supportive environment. When we allow God to be the cornerstone of our families, we are better equipped to navigate the challenges and joys of life together.

In today's scripture, we are reminded that our efforts to build strong families are futile if God is not at the center of our lives. When we invite God into our homes and make Him the foundation of our families, we can experience His guidance, protection, and blessings.

Building a strong family requires effort from all members. It involves open communication, trust, and a commitment to understanding and supporting one another. By creating a loving and nurturing environment, we can foster spiritual growth, emotional well-being, and unity among family members.

Prayer:

Heavenly Father, thank You for the gift of family.

We invite You into our homes and ask that You be the foundation upon which we build our lives. Help us to create a loving, supportive, and nurturing environment that fosters spiritual growth, emotional well-being, and unity among us.

Guide us as we navigate the challenges and joys of life together, and help us to grow closer to You and one another.
May our families be a reflection of Your love, and may we always seek to honor and glorify You in all that we do.

In Jesus' name, we pray. Amen.

Lord Teach Me To

I Am Thankful For

Action Step:

Today, consider how you can invite God into your family life more intentionally.

Whether it's through regular family prayer, Bible study, or worship, make a conscious effort to include God in your daily routines and activities.

Share your thoughts with your family members and discuss ways to strengthen your family's spiritual foundation together.

Day 2: Cultivating Open Communication

Scripture:

"Therefore, having put away falsehood, let each one of you speak the truth with his neighbor, for we are members one of another." - Ephesians 4:25 (ESV)

Reflection:

Open and honest communication is vital to building strong, healthy relationships within a family. When family members feel comfortable sharing their thoughts, feelings, and concerns, it fosters trust, understanding, and unity. It is essential to establish a safe environment where everyone can express themselves without fear of judgment or rejection.

In today's scripture, we are encouraged to speak the truth with one another, as we are all part of the same body. Open communication strengthens family bonds and helps us better understand each other's needs, desires, and perspectives. It also allows us to address and resolve conflicts more effectively.

To cultivate open communication within your family, it is essential to practice active listening and empathy. Be present and attentive when your family members share their thoughts and feelings, and strive to understand their perspective without being judgmental. Encourage honesty and vulnerability by creating a safe space for everyone to express themselves openly.

Prayer:

Heavenly Father, we thank You for the gift of communication. Help us to cultivate open, honest, and empathetic communication within our family.

Teach us to listen attentively to one another, to speak the truth in love, and to create a safe space where everyone can express themselves without fear of judgment or rejection.

May our family be a place of love, support, and understanding, where everyone feels valued and heard. Guide us in our efforts to strengthen our family bonds through open communication, and may we always seek Your wisdom and guidance in our interactions with one another.

In Jesus' name, we pray. Amen.

Lord Teach Me To	**I Am Thankful For**

Action Step:

Set aside dedicated time for family conversations, where everyone has the opportunity to share their thoughts, feelings, and experiences openly.

Practice active listening and empathy, and encourage all family members to do the same.

Consider incorporating regular family meetings or discussion times into your routine to foster ongoing open communication within your family.

Day 3: Making Quality Time a Priority

Scripture:

"Teach us to number our days, that we may gain a heart of wisdom." - Psalm 90:12 (NIV)

Reflection:

In today's fast-paced world, it's easy to become caught up in the busyness of life and lose sight of what truly matters.
One of the most significant gifts we can give our family is the gift of our time. Spending quality time together is essential for nurturing love, understanding, and unity within the family unit.

In today's scripture, we are reminded to be mindful of the time we have and to use it wisely. This wisdom should lead us to prioritize the relationships that matter most – our family. Making quality time a priority creates opportunities for shared experiences, bonding, and making lasting memories.

To make quality time a priority in your family, consider setting aside regular family time for activities that everyone enjoys.
This could include game nights, family meals, outings, or simply spending time together at home. Be intentional about being present and fully engaged during these times, focusing on building connections and strengthening relationships.

Prayer:

Dear Lord, we are grateful for the precious gift of time that You have given us. Help us to be mindful of the time we have and teach us to use it wisely. Guide us in prioritizing quality time with our family and nurturing the relationships that matter most.

Please bless our family time together and fill it with love, joy, and unity. Strengthen our bonds and help us to create lasting memories that we will cherish for a lifetime.
May our family be a source of support, love, and encouragement for one another.

In Jesus' name, we pray. Amen.

Lord Teach Me To

I Am Thankful For

Action Step:

Evaluate your current family schedule and identify any areas where you can create more time for quality family experiences.

Schedule regular family time and be intentional about being present and fully engaged during these moments.

As a family, discuss your favorite activities and create a list of ideas for spending quality time together.

Day 4: Fostering Forgiveness and Reconciliation

Scripture:

"Be kind and compassionate to one another, forgiving each other, just as in Christ God forgave you."
- Ephesians 4:32 (NIV)

Reflection:

In every family, conflicts and misunderstandings are bound to occur. However, the way we handle these challenges is crucial to maintaining strong family bonds. Forgiveness and reconciliation are essential for healing any rifts that might develop within the family unit.

The Bible teaches us that we should be kind, compassionate, and forgiving towards one another, just as God forgives us through Christ. This includes extending forgiveness to our family members, even when it may be difficult. When we choose to forgive, we release ourselves and others from the burden of grudges, bitterness, and resentment.

Fostering forgiveness and reconciliation in the family begins with setting a personal example. As parents or caregivers, we must model a forgiving spirit, teaching our children the importance of extending grace and mercy to others. Encourage open communication within the family, allowing each person to express their feelings and work towards resolving conflicts in a healthy, respectful manner.

Prayer:

Heavenly Father, thank You for the gift of forgiveness that You have extended to us through Your Son, Jesus Christ. Help us to be kind, compassionate, and forgiving toward our family members, just as You are with us.

Please guide us in fostering forgiveness and reconciliation within our family. Give us the strength to let go of any bitterness or resentment, and help us to work together to resolve conflicts in a loving, respectful manner. May our family be a safe and supportive environment where everyone feels heard, valued, and loved.

In Jesus' name, we pray. Amen.

Lord Teach Me To

I Am Thankful For

Action Step:

Reflect on any unresolved conflicts or unresolved feelings within your family.

Take the initiative to address these issues with love and humility, seeking forgiveness and reconciliation.

As a family, discuss the importance of forgiveness and make a commitment to handle conflicts in a respectful, understanding manner.

Day 5: Strengthening Family Through Prayer

Scripture:

"Be kind and compassionate to one another, forgiving each other, just as in Christ God forgave you." - Ephesians 4:32 (NIV)

Reflection:

In every family, conflicts and misunderstandings are bound to occur. However, the way we handle these challenges is crucial to maintaining strong family bonds. Forgiveness and reconciliation are essential for healing any rifts that might develop within the family unit.

The Bible teaches us that we should be kind, compassionate, and forgiving towards one another, just as God forgives us through Christ. This includes extending forgiveness to our family members, even when it may be difficult. When we choose to forgive, we release ourselves and others from the burden of grudges, bitterness, and resentment.

Fostering forgiveness and reconciliation in the family begins with setting a personal example. As parents or caregivers, we must model a forgiving spirit, teaching our children the importance of extending grace and mercy to others. Encourage open communication within the family, allowing each person to express their feelings and work towards resolving conflicts in a healthy, respectful manner.

Prayer:

Heavenly Father, thank You for the gift of forgiveness that You have extended to us through Your Son, Jesus Christ. Help us to be kind, compassionate, and forgiving toward our family members, just as You are with us.

Please guide us in fostering forgiveness and reconciliation within our family. Give us the strength to let go of any bitterness or resentment, and help us to work together to resolve conflicts in a loving, respectful manner. May our family be a safe and supportive environment where everyone feels heard, valued, and loved.

In Jesus' name, we pray. Amen.

Lord Teach Me To

I Am Thankful For

Action Step:

Reflect on any unresolved conflicts or unresolved feelings within your family.

Take the initiative to address these issues with love and humility, seeking forgiveness and reconciliation.

As a family, discuss the importance of forgiveness and make a commitment to handle conflicts in a respectful, understanding manner.

Day 6: Building a Supportive Home Environment

Scripture:

"Let each of you look not only to his own interests, but also to the interests of others." - Philippians 2:4 (NIV)

Reflection:

Creating a supportive home environment is essential for fostering strong family bonds and nurturing the emotional, mental, and spiritual well-being of each family member. A supportive home is a safe haven where love, encouragement, and understanding are abundant, and each person feels valued and accepted.

To build a supportive home environment, start by focusing on open communication, active listening, and empathy. Encourage family members to express their thoughts, feelings, and concerns without fear of judgment or criticism. When someone shares, take the time to listen actively and respond with empathy, offering encouragement and constructive feedback when appropriate.

Promote a sense of teamwork and collaboration within your family by involving everyone in decision-making processes and working together to solve problems or complete tasks. This approach not only fosters cooperation and unity but also helps each person to feel valued and respected for their contributions.

Demonstrate love and support through regular acts of kindness, affirmation, and encouragement. Celebrate the achievements and milestones of each family member, and be there to provide comfort and reassurance during difficult times.

Finally, make it a priority to spend quality time together as a family, engaging in activities that promote bonding, laughter, and connection. This can be as simple as sharing a meal, playing a game, or going for a walk together.

Prayer:

Heavenly Father, we ask for Your guidance and wisdom as we strive to create a supportive home environment for our family.
Help us to cultivate open communication, active listening, and empathy, and teach us to value and respect the needs and interests of each family member.

May our home be a place of love, encouragement, and understanding, where each person feels cherished and supported.
We pray that You would bless our efforts to strengthen our family bonds and nurture the emotional, mental, and spiritual well-being of each family member.

In Jesus' name, we pray. Amen.

Lord Teach Me To

I Am Thankful For

Action Step:

Identify one area of your home environment that could benefit from greater support and encouragement.

Discuss this area with your family members and work together to create a plan for improvement.

Be intentional in your efforts to promote open communication, active listening, and empathy, and prioritize spending quality time together as a family.

Day 7: The Importance of Family Traditions

Scripture:

"Train up a child in the way he should go; even when he is old he will not depart from it." - Proverbs 22:6 (NIV)

Reflection:

Family traditions are powerful tools for strengthening family bonds and creating a sense of unity and belonging. They provide a foundation for shared experiences, memories, and values that can be passed down from one generation to the next. Family traditions help to establish a sense of identity and give family members a sense of stability, continuity, and predictability.

To create meaningful family traditions, consider the following steps:

- **Reflect on your family's values and priorities.** What beliefs, values, or experiences do you want to pass down to your children and future generations? Use these insights to guide the development of your family traditions.
- **Involve all family members in the planning and implementation of traditions.** Encourage each person to contribute their ideas, interests, and talents, and be open to new ideas and perspectives.
- **Be intentional about incorporating your family's unique culture, history, and heritage into your traditions.** This can help to foster a deeper sense of belonging and identity among family members.
- **Ensure that your traditions are flexible and adaptable, allowing for changes and growth within your family.** As children grow and new family members join, be open to adjusting or expanding your traditions to accommodate these changes.
- **Remember that the goal of family traditions is to strengthen your family bonds, not to create additional stress or obligations.** Keep your traditions simple, enjoyable, and meaningful for everyone involved.

Prayer:

Dear Lord, we thank You for the gift of family and the opportunity to create meaningful traditions that will strengthen our bonds and nurture our shared values. Guide us in developing traditions that reflect our family's unique culture, history, and heritage, and help us to create memories that will last a lifetime.

We ask for Your wisdom and discernment as we seek to balance the demands of daily life with our desire to create a sense of unity and belonging within our family. In all that we do, may our family traditions bring glory to Your name and draw us closer to one another and to You.

In Jesus' name, we pray. Amen.

Lord Teach Me To

I Am Thankful For

Action Step:

Take some time this week to discuss your family's current traditions and brainstorm ideas for new traditions that reflect your shared values and priorities.

Be sure to involve all family members in the planning process, and make an effort to incorporate your family's unique culture, history, and heritage into your traditions.

Day 8: Developing Healthy Boundaries

Scripture:

"Above all else, guard your heart, for everything you do flows from it." - Proverbs 4:23 (NIV)

Reflection:

Healthy boundaries are essential for maintaining strong, loving relationships within a family. They provide a framework for understanding and respecting each individual's needs, feelings, and perspectives, while fostering a sense of safety and trust. Boundaries help to create a balance between individual autonomy and family unity, allowing each family member to grow and flourish in their unique way.

To develop healthy boundaries within your family, consider the following steps:

- **Communicate openly and honestly about your needs and feelings.** Encourage each family member to express their thoughts and emotions in a respectful, non-judgmental manner, and listen actively to one another's perspectives.
- **Set clear expectations for behavior and responsibilities within the family.** Establish guidelines for how family members should treat one another, and outline the roles and responsibilities of each individual within the family unit.
- **Respect each family member's right to privacy and personal space.** Allow for individual time and space, and acknowledge that each person has the right to their own thoughts, feelings, and experiences.
- **Be consistent in enforcing boundaries and consequences.** When a boundary has been crossed, address the issue promptly and calmly, and follow through with any agreed-upon consequences.
- **Be willing to reassess and adjust boundaries as needed.** As family members grow and change, it may be necessary to reevaluate and adjust boundaries to accommodate new needs and circumstances.

Prayer:

Dear Heavenly Father, thank You for the gift of family and the opportunity to grow together in love and unity. Help us to develop healthy boundaries within our family, so that each individual can feel valued, respected, and safe.

We ask for Your guidance and wisdom as we navigate the complexities of family life, and we pray that our relationships will be strengthened and enriched by our efforts to establish and maintain healthy boundaries. May our family be a place of love, support, and encouragement, where each individual can grow and flourish in their unique way, and may we always be mindful of Your presence in our lives.

In Jesus' name, we pray. Amen.

Lord Teach Me To

I Am Thankful For

Action Step:

This week, have a family discussion about the importance of healthy boundaries and explore ways to establish or strengthen boundaries within your family.

Encourage open communication, and work together to identify areas where boundaries may need to be reassessed or adjusted.

Day 9: The Power of Parental Leadership

Scripture:

"Train up a child in the way he should go; even when he is old he will not depart from it." - Proverbs 22:6 (NIV)

Reflection:

Parental leadership plays a crucial role in shaping the character and values of a family. As parents, you have the unique opportunity and responsibility to guide your children and provide a strong foundation for their growth and development. By modeling positive behaviors, teaching essential life skills, and fostering open communication, you can create a nurturing environment that supports the well-being and success of your family.

Here are some tips to help you embrace your role as a parental leader:

- **Model the values and behaviors you want to instill in your children.** Children learn by example, so strive to demonstrate the qualities you hope to see in your children, such as kindness, honesty, and respect.
- **Foster a safe and loving environment at home.** Create a supportive atmosphere where your children feel comfortable sharing their thoughts, feelings, and experiences without fear of judgment or rejection.
- **Encourage your children to develop a strong moral compass.** Teach them the importance of empathy, compassion, and integrity, and provide guidance on making ethical choices.
- **Support your children's interests and talents.** Encourage them to pursue their passions, and provide the necessary resources and opportunities for them to develop their skills and abilities.
- **Set realistic expectations and consequences.** Establish clear expectations for behavior and performance, and enforce appropriate consequences when necessary.
- **Foster resilience and perseverance.** Teach your children the importance of facing challenges and setbacks with courage, determination, and a positive attitude.

Prayer:

Dear Heavenly Father, thank You for entrusting us with the responsibility of raising our children. Help us to be strong, loving, and wise parental leaders, guiding our children with Your love and grace.

Grant us the wisdom and patience to teach our children the values and principles that will help them grow into compassionate, responsible, and faithful individuals. Help us to create a home environment where they feel loved, supported, and inspired to reach their full potential.
We pray for Your guidance and strength as we navigate the challenges and joys of parenthood, and we ask that You would bless our efforts to lead our family in a way that honors You.

In Jesus' name, we pray. Amen.

Lord Teach Me To	I Am Thankful For

Action Step:

This week, take time to reflect on your role as a parental leader in your family.

Consider ways you can improve your leadership skills and better support the growth and development of your children.

Commit to making a conscious effort to model the values and behaviors you want to instill in your children.

Day 10: Sibling Bonds and Relationships

Scripture:

"How good and pleasant it is when God's people live together in unity!" - Psalm 133:1 (NIV)

Reflection:

Sibling relationships are an essential component of a strong and loving family unit. The bonds between brothers and sisters can provide a foundation for lifelong friendships and support, contributing to emotional well-being and personal growth. By fostering healthy sibling relationships, parents can help create a positive family atmosphere that nurtures love, trust, and cooperation.

Here are some tips to encourage positive sibling bonds:

-Encourage open communication. Teach your children the importance of expressing their feelings and thoughts with one another, fostering empathy and understanding.

- Set clear expectations for respectful behavior. Establish rules and guidelines for how siblings should treat each other, emphasizing kindness, respect, and patience.

- Foster a spirit of cooperation and teamwork. Encourage your children to work together on projects or chores, emphasizing the importance of collaboration and problem-solving.

- Celebrate individuality. Recognize and appreciate each child's unique qualities, strengths, and interests, and encourage them to support and celebrate one another's achievements and successes.

- Encourage conflict resolution. Teach your children healthy strategies for resolving disagreements and conflicts, such as active listening, compromise, and taking turns speaking.

- Model positive sibling relationships. Demonstrate healthy and loving relationships with your own siblings, if applicable, to show your children the value of strong sibling bonds.

Prayer:

Heavenly Father, thank You for the gift of family and the special relationships between siblings. We ask that You bless and strengthen the bonds between our children, helping them to develop a deep love, respect, and understanding for one another.

Guide us, Lord, as we strive to create a loving and supportive environment where our children can grow and thrive together. Help us to teach them the importance of unity, cooperation, and empathy, and to model the kind of sibling relationships that honor You.

We pray that You would watch over and protect our children as they navigate the joys and challenges of their sibling relationships, and that their bonds would grow stronger with each passing day.

In Jesus' name, we pray. Amen.

Lord Teach Me To

I Am Thankful For

Action Step:

This week, take time to observe the interactions between your children and identify areas where you can help foster healthier sibling relationships.

Encourage open communication and teamwork, and model positive sibling interactions within your family.

Day 11: Encouraging Emotional Intelligence

Scripture:

"Be completely humble and gentle; be patient, bearing with one another in love." - Ephesians 4:2 (NIV)

Reflection:

Emotional intelligence is the ability to recognize, understand, and manage our own emotions as well as the emotions of others. It plays a crucial role in fostering healthy relationships within families and is essential for maintaining harmony and unity among family members. Encouraging emotional intelligence in your children helps them to develop empathy, self-awareness, and effective communication skills, which are vital for nurturing strong family bonds.

Here are some ways to encourage emotional intelligence in your family:
-**Teach emotional vocabulary:** Help your children to identify and name their emotions, such as anger, happiness, sadness, or frustration. This will enable them to express themselves more effectively and develop a better understanding of their feelings.
- **Validate emotions:** Encourage your children to express their emotions openly, and validate their feelings by showing empathy and understanding. Let them know that it's okay to feel a certain way and that their emotions are normal.
- **Model emotional intelligence:** Demonstrate healthy emotional expression and self-regulation in your own behavior. Show your children how to recognize and manage their emotions by setting a positive example.
- **Encourage empathy:** Teach your children to put themselves in others' shoes and consider their feelings. This will help them to develop compassion and understanding towards their siblings and other family members.
- **Teach problem-solving:** Help your children to identify the cause of their emotions and find appropriate solutions to their problems. This will empower them to take control of their emotions and improve their relationships with others.

Prayer:

Heavenly Father, we thank You for the gift of emotional intelligence and its role in creating strong, loving families. We ask that You help us to foster emotional intelligence within our family, enabling our children to develop empathy, self-awareness, and effective communication skills. Guide us, Lord, as we seek to model healthy emotional expression and self-regulation for our children. Help us to validate their emotions, encourage empathy, and teach problem-solving skills that will empower them to navigate their relationships with grace and understanding.

We pray that You would bless our efforts to cultivate emotional intelligence within our family and that our children would grow into emotionally healthy, compassionate individuals who honor You in their relationships.

In Jesus' name, we pray. Amen.

Lord Teach Me To

I Am Thankful For

Action Step:

This week, focus on encouraging emotional intelligence within your family.

Teach your children to identify and name their emotions, validate their feelings, and model healthy emotional expression.

Foster empathy and compassion among family members, and guide your children in developing problem-solving skills to help them manage their emotions effectively.

Day 12: Nurturing Spiritual Growth in Children

Scripture:

"Train up a child in the way he should go; even when he is old he will not depart from it." - Proverbs 22:6 (NIV)

Reflection:

Spiritual growth is an essential aspect of a child's overall development and well-being. Nurturing your children's spiritual growth will help them develop a strong foundation of faith and a personal relationship with God. It will also guide them in making wise choices, finding purpose and direction in life, and experiencing God's love, grace, and forgiveness.

Here are some ways to nurture spiritual growth in your children:

-**Create a God-centered home:** Make God the center of your family life by incorporating faith-based practices, such as prayer, Bible reading, and worship, into your daily routine.
- **Teach them about God and the Bible:** Share Bible stories, teachings, and principles with your children in age-appropriate ways. Encourage their curiosity and allow them to ask questions about faith, God, and the Bible.
- **Pray with and for your children:** Pray together as a family and teach your children the importance and power of prayer. Encourage them to develop a personal prayer life and to bring their concerns and thanksgivings to God.
- **Model a Christ-like life:** Live out your faith through your actions, words, and relationships. Set a positive example for your children by demonstrating love, forgiveness, and grace in your own life.
- **Encourage involvement in a faith community:** Participate in a local church or faith-based community where your children can learn from others, grow in their faith, and serve others.

Prayer:

Heavenly Father, thank You for the precious gift of our children and the opportunity to nurture their spiritual growth. We ask for Your guidance and wisdom as we seek to lead them in developing a personal relationship with You and a strong foundation of faith.

Help us, Lord, to create a God-centered home where our children can experience Your love, grace, and forgiveness. Teach us how to share Your Word with them in ways that they can understand and embrace.

We pray that You would empower us to model a Christ-like life for our children and that our family would be a living testimony of Your love and goodness. May our children grow to love and serve You with all their hearts, minds, and souls.

In Jesus' name, we pray. Amen.

Lord Teach Me To	I Am Thankful For

Action Step:

This week, focus on nurturing your children's spiritual growth. Create a God-centered home, teach them about God and the Bible, pray with and for them, model a Christ-like life, and encourage involvement in a faith community.

Be intentional in guiding your children to develop a strong foundation of faith and a personal relationship with God.

Day 13: Overcoming Challenges as a Family

Scripture:

"Consider it pure joy, my brothers and sisters, whenever you face trials of many kinds, because you know that the testing of your faith produces perseverance." - James 1:2-3 (NIV)

Reflection:

Every family faces challenges and struggles at some point in their journey. These difficulties can range from financial stress, health issues, to conflicts and misunderstandings. Overcoming these challenges together as a family not only strengthens your relationships but also deepens your faith and reliance on God.

Here are some ways to overcome challenges as a family:

- **Communicate openly and honestly:** Encourage open and honest communication among family members. Share your feelings, concerns, and experiences, and listen to each other with empathy and understanding.
- **Pray together:** Prayer is a powerful tool to help families face their challenges. Pray together as a family, bringing your concerns, needs, and thanksgivings to God. Trust in His divine intervention and guidance.
- **Support and encourage one another:** Offer emotional support to each other, especially during difficult times. Be there for each other, offer a listening ear, and provide words of encouragement and hope.
- **Work together to find solutions:** Face challenges together as a team and brainstorm solutions. Encourage each family member to contribute their ideas, perspectives, and strengths to overcome the obstacle.
- **Learn and grow from the experience:** View challenges as opportunities for growth and learning. Reflect on the lessons learned and the ways in which your family has grown stronger and more resilient.
- **Seek professional help if necessary:** Sometimes, challenges may require outside assistance, such as counseling, financial advice, or medical intervention. Do not hesitate to seek professional help when needed.

Prayer:

Dear Lord, we thank You for the gift of family and the love and support that we share. We know that challenges and struggles are a part of life, and we ask for Your guidance and strength as we face them together.
Help us to communicate openly and honestly, support and encourage one another, and work together to find solutions to our challenges.
We pray that You would teach us valuable lessons through these experiences and help us grow stronger as a family.
Grant us the wisdom to seek professional help when necessary, and provide us with the resources we need to overcome our challenges. May we always trust in Your love, provision, and faithfulness, even during the most difficult times.

In Jesus' name, we pray. Amen.

Lord Teach Me To	I Am Thankful For

Action Step:

This week, identify a challenge that your family is currently facing.

Work together to communicate openly, support one another, and find solutions to overcome the challenge.

Pray together, learn from the experience, and seek professional help if needed.

Day 14: The Value of Family Rituals

Scripture:

"You shall love the Lord your God with all your heart and with all your soul and with all your might. And these words that I command you today shall be on your heart.
You shall teach them diligently to your children, and shall talk of them when you sit in your house, and when you walk by the way, and when you lie down, and when you rise." - Deuteronomy 6:5-7 (ESV)

Reflection:

Family rituals are simple, recurring activities that carry special meaning for the members of the family. These rituals can help create a sense of belonging, strengthen family bonds, and promote a shared identity. They also provide opportunities for families to connect on a deeper level, pass on values and beliefs, and create lasting memories.

Here are some examples of family rituals:

- **Family meals:** Sharing meals together provides an opportunity for family members to connect, communicate, and share their daily experiences. Make an effort to have regular family meals, free from distractions like electronic devices.
- **Bedtime routines:** Establish a consistent bedtime routine that includes reading, prayers, or sharing the day's highlights. This helps children feel safe and secure while providing a time for bonding and connection.
- **Celebrations and traditions:** Celebrate special occasions, such as birthdays, anniversaries, and holidays, with unique family traditions. These celebrations can include special meals, activities, or rituals that are meaningful to your family.
- **Acts of service:** Engage in regular acts of service as a family, such as volunteering at a local food bank or participating in community clean-up projects. This fosters a spirit of generosity and empathy within the family.
- **Spiritual practices:** Incorporate spiritual practices into your family's daily life, such as prayer, reading Scripture, or attending worship services together. This helps to nurture the spiritual growth and well-being of your family.

Prayer:

Heavenly Father, we thank You for the gift of family and the special bonds that we share. We ask that You guide us in creating meaningful family rituals that strengthen our connections, nurture our faith, and enrich our lives.

Help us to be intentional in carving out time for these rituals amidst our busy schedules. May they become cherished memories that we carry with us throughout our lives.

We pray that our family rituals will not only bring us closer together but also draw us closer to You. May they serve as a reminder of Your love, grace, and presence in our lives.

In Jesus' name, we pray. Amen.

Lord Teach Me To

I Am Thankful For

Action Step:

This week, reflect on your family's current rituals and traditions.

Consider incorporating new rituals that align with your family's values and beliefs.

Make a commitment to prioritize these rituals, and enjoy the benefits of strengthened family bonds and a deeper connection with one another.

Day 15: Building Trust and Reliability

Scripture:

"Whoever walks in integrity walks securely, but he who makes his ways crooked will be found out." - Proverbs 10:9 (ESV)

Reflection:

Trust is the foundation of any strong relationship, and it is especially crucial in family dynamics. When family members trust each other, they feel safe, secure, and supported. Building trust within a family takes time, effort, and consistency. It requires a commitment to being reliable, honest, and accountable.

Here are some ways to build trust and reliability within your family:

- **Keep promises:** Make a conscious effort to follow through on the promises you make to your family members. This demonstrates your commitment to them and shows that they can depend on you.
- **Be consistent**: Consistency in your actions and behavior helps create a sense of stability and predictability within the family. This, in turn, fosters trust as family members know what to expect from one another.
- **Communicate openly and honestly:** Encourage open and honest communication within your family. Share your feelings, thoughts, and experiences, and listen attentively when others do the same. This helps to create a safe space where trust can grow.
- **Apologize and forgive:** When you make mistakes or hurt someone's feelings, take responsibility for your actions, and apologize sincerely. Likewise, be willing to forgive others when they apologize to you. This demonstrates humility, fosters understanding, and helps to rebuild trust.
- **Show support:** Be there for your family members when they need you, whether it's offering a listening ear, a word of encouragement, or a helping hand. This shows that you care and are committed to their well-being.

Prayer:

Heavenly Father, thank You for the blessing of family and the opportunity to grow together in love and trust. Help us to be mindful of our actions and words, striving to be reliable, honest, and accountable to one another.

Teach us the importance of open communication, forgiveness, and support as we work to build trust within our family. May our actions reflect Your love and grace, fostering an environment of trust, security, and unity.

We pray that our family relationships will be strengthened by our commitment to trust and reliability, and that through these efforts, our bonds will deepen and our love for one another will grow.

In Jesus' name, we pray. Amen.

Lord Teach Me To	I Am Thankful For

Action Step:

This week, focus on the ways in which you can build trust and reliability within your family.

Be intentional about keeping promises, communicating openly, and offering support to your family members.

As you work to strengthen trust, observe how it positively impacts your family dynamics and relationships.

Day 16: Cultivating Empathy and Compassion

Scripture:

"Be kind and compassionate to one another, forgiving each other, just as in Christ God forgave you." - Ephesians 4:32 (NIV)

Reflection:

Empathy and compassion are essential qualities for nurturing strong, healthy relationships within a family. When we are empathetic, we can understand and share the feelings of others. Compassion, on the other hand, is the desire to alleviate the suffering of others. By cultivating these qualities in our families, we can create an environment where each member feels seen, heard, and valued.

Here are some ways to cultivate empathy and compassion within your family:

- **Practice active listening:** When a family member speaks, make a conscious effort to listen without interrupting or forming judgments. This helps to create a safe space where individuals feel comfortable sharing their thoughts and emotions.
- **Encourage perspective-taking:** Help your family members understand the feelings and experiences of others by discussing different perspectives. This can help to build empathy and promote understanding.
- **Model empathy and compassion:** Demonstrate empathy and compassion in your actions and words, both within your family and with others. This sets a powerful example for your family members to follow.
- **Offer support and assistance:** When a family member is going through a challenging time, offer support and assistance as needed. This not only helps to alleviate their burden but also fosters compassion within the family.
- **Share stories of empathy and compassion:** Discuss real-life examples or stories that demonstrate empathy and compassion, either from your own experiences or from the media. This can help to reinforce the importance of these qualities in family life.

Prayer:

Heavenly Father, thank You for the gift of empathy and compassion. We ask that You help us to cultivate these qualities within our family so that we can better understand and support one another.

Teach us to be active listeners and to consider the perspectives of others. Guide us in modeling empathy and compassion for our family members, and open our hearts to the needs of those around us.

We pray that our family will be a safe and nurturing space where each member feels seen, heard, and valued. May our empathy and compassion strengthen our bonds and deepen our love for one another.

In Jesus' name, we pray. Amen.

Lord Teach Me To

I Am Thankful For

Action Step:

This week, make a conscious effort to practice empathy and compassion within your family.

Listen actively to your family members, encourage perspective-taking, and offer support as needed.

Reflect on the impact of these actions on your family relationships and dynamics.

Day 17: Establishing Family Goals and Values

Scripture:

"Train up a child in the way he should go; even when he is old, he will not depart from it." - Proverbs 22:6 (NIV)

Reflection:

Family goals and values provide a foundation upon which strong and unified families are built. By establishing shared goals and values, your family can work together towards common objectives, while fostering a sense of belonging and purpose for each member. Moreover, clear family values can serve as guiding principles that inform decision-making and shape behavior within the family.

Here are some steps to help you establish family goals and values:

- **Reflect on your current family values:** Consider the values that are important to you and your family members. These may include love, honesty, respect, kindness, responsibility, or faith.
- **Involve everyone in the process:** Encourage each family member to share their thoughts on what they believe are essential values for the family. This promotes a sense of ownership and buy-in from all members.
- **Prioritize your values:** Once you have identified your family values, prioritize them according to their importance. This will help to provide a clear focus for your family as you move forward.
- **Set family goals:** Based on your prioritized values, set specific and achievable goals for your family. These goals should be aligned with your values and should help to strengthen your family bonds.
- **Regularly review and update:** As your family grows and changes, it is essential to revisit your family goals and values regularly. This ensures that they continue to be relevant and meaningful for your family.

Prayer:

Heavenly Father, thank You for the gift of family. We ask for Your guidance as we seek to establish our family goals and values. Help us to identify the values that are most important to us and to prioritize them in a way that honors You.

Grant us the wisdom and strength to set achievable family goals that align with our values and strengthen our bonds. May our family be a living example of Your love, grace, and mercy, and may our goals and values reflect Your divine plan for us.

In Jesus' name, we pray. Amen.

Lord Teach Me To

I Am Thankful For

Action Step:

This week, take time to reflect on your current family values and discuss them with your family members.

Together, prioritize these values and set specific family goals based on them.

Regularly review and update your family goals and values to ensure they continue to be relevant and meaningful.

Day 18: Balancing Family, Work, and Leisure

Scripture:

"Be very careful, then, how you live—not as unwise but as wise, making the most of every opportunity, because the days are evil."
- Ephesians 5:15-16 (NIV)

Reflection:

Achieving balance between family, work, and leisure is essential for maintaining harmony and well-being in our lives. It's important to nurture each of these aspects, as they contribute to our overall happiness and fulfillment. However, finding the right balance can be challenging, especially in today's fast-paced world.

Here are some tips for balancing family, work, and leisure:

- **Set priorities:** Determine what is most important to you in each area of your life, and make sure you allocate time and energy accordingly. This may require some adjustments and sacrifices, but having clear priorities will help you make more intentional choices.
- **Schedule family time:** Just as you schedule work meetings and appointments, be intentional about scheduling quality family time. Set aside regular time for family activities, meals, and bonding.
- **Establish boundaries:** Establish clear boundaries between work and family life. When you're at work, focus on your tasks and responsibilities; when you're at home, devote your attention to your family. Avoid bringing work-related stress into your family life and vice versa.
- **Communicate with your partner:** Open communication with your spouse or partner is crucial for maintaining balance. Discuss your schedules, expectations, and any challenges you may be facing, and work together to find solutions.
- **Make time for leisure:** Don't forget to allocate time for hobbies, relaxation, and self-care. Engaging in leisure activities not only helps to relieve stress but also enables you to be more present and attentive when you're with your family.

Prayer:

Dear Lord, thank You for the many blessings You have bestowed upon us, including our families, work, and leisure time. We ask for Your guidance as we strive to find balance among these areas of our lives. Help us to prioritize our time and energy in a way that honors You and nurtures our relationships.

Grant us the wisdom to establish healthy boundaries between work and family life, and the discipline to stick to them. May our families be a source of joy, love, and support, and may our work be a reflection of our commitment to serve You.

In Jesus' name, we pray. Amen.

Lord Teach Me To	I Am Thankful For

Action Step:

This week, evaluate how you're currently balancing family, work, and leisure.

Consider what adjustments you may need to make, and implement changes to help create a healthier balance.

Prioritize family time, establish boundaries, communicate with your partner, and make time for leisure activities to ensure a well-rounded life.

Day 19: Creating a Culture of Service

Scripture:

"But be sure to fear the Lord and serve Him faithfully with all your heart; consider what great things He has done for you." - 1 Samuel 12:24 (NIV)

Reflection:

Serving others is a core principle of Christianity. Jesus Himself exemplified service through His life, teachings, and ultimate sacrifice on the cross. By creating a culture of service within our families, we can pass on these values to our children and strengthen our family bonds.

Here are some tips for creating a culture of service in your family:

- **Lead by example:** As a parent or guardian, demonstrate a heart of service in your own actions. When your children see you helping others and being kind, they will be more likely to follow in your footsteps.
- **Encourage acts of kindness:** Praise and encourage your children when they display acts of kindness and service, both within the family and in the broader community. Acknowledge their efforts and reinforce the importance of helping others.
- **Engage in family service projects:** Choose service projects or volunteer opportunities that your whole family can participate in together. This can include supporting a local food bank, participating in a community clean-up, or helping a neighbor in need.
- **Discuss the importance of service:** Talk openly with your children about the value of serving others and the impact it has on individuals and the community. Share stories from your own experiences and from the lives of others who have made a difference through service.
- **Foster empathy and compassion:** Teach your children to empathize with the needs and feelings of others. Encourage them to put themselves in someone else's shoes and consider how they might feel in a similar situation.

Prayer:

Heavenly Father, thank You for the example of service that Jesus provided during His time on Earth.
We ask that You help us instill a culture of service within our families, allowing us to grow closer to one another and to You.

Guide us as we teach our children the importance of serving others and helping those in need.
May we lead by example, showing kindness and compassion in our every-day lives. We pray that our family's service to others would be a light in our community and a reflection of Your love.

In Jesus' name, we pray. Amen.

Lord Teach Me To

I Am Thankful For

Action Step:

This week, discuss the concept of service with your family and brainstorm ways to engage in acts of service together.
Choose one or more service projects or volunteer opportunities to participate in as a family, and make a plan to follow through on these commitments.
Encourage your children to look for ways to serve others in their daily lives, and praise them when they demonstrate acts of kindness and service.

Day 20: The Role of Faith in Family Life

Scripture:

"Train up a child in the way he should go; even when he is old he will not depart from it." - Proverbs 22:6 (ESV)

Reflection:

Faith plays a crucial role in nurturing a strong and loving family. As parents and guardians, it is our responsibility to instill a solid foundation of faith within our children and to create an environment where our family's spiritual life can flourish. Integrating faith into family life helps to create a sense of purpose, fosters moral values, and teaches the importance of relying on God in all aspects of life.

Here are some ways to incorporate faith into your family life:

- **Make prayer a daily habit:** Set aside time each day for family prayer. This can include a morning devotional, mealtime blessings, or bedtime prayers. Encourage your children to share their prayer requests and thanksgivings, fostering open communication with God and each other.

- **Attend worship services together:** Regularly attending worship services as a family can help to establish a sense of community and belonging within your faith community. Engage in discussions about the sermon or worship experience, and encourage your children to participate in age-appropriate activities or groups within your church or religious organization.

- **Study scripture together:** Set aside time each week for family Bible study or scripture reading. Encourage your children to ask questions and share their thoughts as you explore God's Word together. This can also serve as an opportunity to teach them about the history and teachings of your faith tradition.

- **Serve together:** Engage in acts of service as a family, both within your faith community and in the broader community. Serving others not only strengthens family bonds but also allows you to live out your faith in tangible ways.

- **Share your faith journey:** Share stories of your personal faith journey with your children, including challenges, victories, and moments of growth. This openness can help to build trust and understanding within the family and encourage your children to share their own experiences and questions about faith.

Prayer:

Heavenly Father, we thank You for the gift of family and the opportunity to grow together in faith. We ask that You guide us as we seek to nurture our family's spiritual life and create an environment where faith can flourish.

Help us to be intentional in our efforts to teach our children about Your love, Your Word, and Your ways.

May our family be a beacon of light and hope in our community, and may our faith be a firm foundation for all that we do.

In Jesus' name, we pray. Amen.

Lord Teach Me To	I Am Thankful For

Action Step:

This week, make a conscious effort to incorporate faith into your family's daily life. Set aside time for prayer, attend worship services together, and engage in family Bible study or scripture reading.

Share your personal faith journey with your children and encourage open discussions about faith and spiritual growth.

Finally, look for opportunities to serve together as a family, both within your faith community and in the broader community.

Day 21: Resolving Conflicts with Love and Respect

Scripture:

"A soft answer turns away wrath, but a harsh word stirs up anger." - Proverbs 15:1 (ESV)

Reflection:

Conflicts are a natural part of family life. As individuals with unique personalities, perspectives, and emotions, disagreements are bound to arise. However, it's not the conflicts themselves that can damage relationships, but rather the way we handle them. Approaching conflicts with love and respect is essential to fostering a healthy and supportive family environment.

Here are some tips for resolving conflicts with love and respect:

- **Practice active listening:** When a disagreement arises, make an effort to genuinely listen to each other's concerns and feelings. Avoid interrupting or becoming defensive. Instead, show empathy and strive to understand the other person's point of view.

- **Use "I" statements:** Express your feelings and thoughts by using "I" statements, which focus on your emotions and experiences, rather than blaming or accusing the other person. This can help to prevent defensiveness and promote open communication.

- **Be mindful of your tone:** The way you speak to one another during a conflict can significantly impact the outcome. Speak calmly and respectfully, avoiding raised voices or harsh words. Remember that it's possible to express your feelings and concerns without being confrontational.

- **Seek a compromise:** When appropriate, seek a compromise that takes into account the needs and desires of all parties involved. This may involve some give and take, but it demonstrates a willingness to prioritize the relationship over personal preferences.

- **Apologize and forgive:** Be willing to apologize when you've hurt or wronged someone and be open to forgiving others when they've hurt or wronged you. Holding onto grudges can lead to bitterness and resentment, which can damage the family bond.

- **Pray for guidance:** When conflicts arise, turn to God for guidance and wisdom. Pray for the ability to approach disagreements with love, patience, and understanding.

Prayer:

Heavenly Father, we know that conflicts are a part of life, but we ask for Your guidance and wisdom as we navigate them within our family. Help us to approach disagreements with love, respect, and a desire for understanding.

Grant us the patience to listen, the humility to apologize and forgive, and the wisdom to seek compromises that honor You and strengthen our family bonds. May our relationships be a testament to Your love and grace, and may we grow together in unity and love.

In Jesus' name, we pray. Amen.

Lord Teach Me To	I Am Thankful For

Action Step:

This week, be mindful of how you handle conflicts within your family.

Practice active listening, use "I" statements, and be conscious of your tone. Seek compromises and be willing to apologize and forgive.

Finally, turn to God in prayer for guidance and wisdom in navigating disagreements with love and respect.

Day 22: Learning to Listen and Understand

Scripture:

"Know this, my beloved brothers: let every person be quick to hear, slow to speak, slow to anger." - James 1:19 (ESV)

Reflection:

Effective communication is the foundation of strong relationships, and listening is an essential part of that process. In a world filled with distractions, it can be challenging to genuinely listen and understand our family members. However, by making an effort to be fully present and attentive, we can strengthen our connections and foster a deeper understanding of one another.

Here are some strategies for learning to listen and understand:

- **Be fully present:** When engaging in a conversation, eliminate distractions and focus on the person you're speaking with. Put away your phone, turn off the TV, and give your full attention to the conversation.

- **Be patient:** Allow the other person to speak without interrupting them. Resist the urge to jump in with your thoughts or solutions immediately. Give them the time and space to express themselves fully.

- **Show empathy:** Try to put yourself in the other person's shoes and understand their feelings and perspective. Respond with empathy and compassion, even if you don't agree with what they're saying.

- **Ask open-ended questions:** Encourage deeper conversation by asking open-ended questions that invite the other person to share more about their thoughts and feelings.

- **Reflect back what you hear:** Summarize and paraphrase what the other person has said to ensure you've understood them correctly. This also demonstrates that you've been actively listening and value their thoughts and feelings.

- **Avoid judgment:** Approach conversations with an open mind and a willingness to learn from the other person's perspective. Avoid passing judgment or making assumptions about their experiences.

- **Pray for understanding:** Ask God to help you become a better listener and to grant you the wisdom and understanding needed to truly hear and empathize with your family members.

Prayer:

Heavenly Father, thank You for the gift of family and the opportunity to grow together in love and understanding. Help us to become better listeners, to be fully present in our conversations, and to approach each interaction with empathy and compassion.

Grant us the patience to listen without interrupting, the wisdom to ask meaningful questions, and the humility to avoid judgment.

May our communication be a reflection of Your love and grace, drawing us closer together as a family and deepening our relationships.

In Jesus' name, we pray. Amen.

Lord Teach Me To

I Am Thankful For

Action Step:

This week, practice the strategies for effective listening in your conversations with family members.

Be fully present, patient, empathetic, and open-minded. Pray for God's guidance in becoming a better listener and deepening your understanding of your loved ones.

Day 23: Celebrating Individuality and Uniqueness

Scripture:

"For you created my inmost being; you knit me together in my mother's womb. I praise you because I am fearfully and wonderfully made; your works are wonderful, I know that full well." - Psalm 139:13-14 (NIV)

Reflection:

Every family is made up of unique individuals, each with their own talents, personalities, and quirks. Embracing and celebrating these differences is an essential part of nurturing a strong and loving family unit. When we appreciate and honor each other's individuality, we create an environment where everyone can thrive and grow into the people God intended them to be.

Here are some ways to celebrate individuality and uniqueness within your family:

- **Encourage personal growth:** Support each family member in pursuing their interests, goals, and dreams. Provide opportunities for them to explore new activities and develop their skills.
- **Recognize strengths:** Acknowledge and celebrate the unique strengths and talents of each family member. Encourage them to use their gifts to contribute to the family and the world around them.
- **Foster self-expression:** Create a safe space for family members to express their thoughts, feelings, and opinions without fear of judgment or criticism. Encourage open and honest communication.
- **Value differences:** Teach your family to appreciate the diversity of the human experience and to respect the perspectives and experiences of others. Model this behavior by showing kindness and understanding towards others who are different from you.
- **Create family traditions:** Develop family traditions that honor the uniqueness of each family member. These can be simple things like celebrating each person's favorite meal on their birthday or creating a family memory book filled with stories and pictures of each individual.
- **Pray for one another:** Make it a habit to pray for each family member, asking God to bless them and help them grow into the person He created them to be.

Prayer:

Dear Lord, thank You for creating each one of us with unique gifts, talents, and personalities. Help us to appreciate and celebrate the individuality of each member of our family. Teach us to support and encourage one another in our personal growth and self-expression.

Grant us the wisdom to value and respect our differences, and guide us in nurturing a loving and supportive family environment where everyone can thrive.
May we always remember that we are fearfully and wonderfully made by You.

In Jesus' name, we pray. Amen.

Lord Teach Me To	I Am Thankful For

Action Step:

This week, make an effort to acknowledge and celebrate the individuality of each family member.

Encourage their personal growth, recognize their strengths, and foster an atmosphere of love and acceptance.

Pray for God's guidance in helping you create a strong and loving family that values the uniqueness of each person.

Day 24: The Power of Unconditional Love

Scripture:

"Love is patient, love is kind. It does not envy, it does not boast, it is not proud. It does not dishonor others, it is not self-seeking, it is not easily angered, it keeps no record of wrongs. Love does not delight in evil but rejoices with the truth. It always protects, always trusts, always hopes, always perseveres. Love never fails." - 1 Corinthians 13:4-8 (NIV)

Reflection:

Unconditional love is a powerful force that can transform families and create a strong foundation for nurturing love and unity. It means loving your family members without judgment, expectation, or condition, accepting and cherishing them for who they are. Unconditional love is the embodiment of the love that God has for each of us, and it is our calling to share this love with our families.

Here are some ways to practice unconditional love in your family:

- **Acceptance:** Embrace your family members as they are, without trying to change or control them. Recognize their individuality and uniqueness, and appreciate the qualities that make them special.
- **Forgiveness:** Learn to forgive the mistakes and shortcomings of your family members. Remember that everyone is human and that we all make mistakes. Choose to let go of grudges and resentments and move forward with love.
- **Encouragement:** Support and encourage your family members in their personal growth and development. Celebrate their achievements and help them overcome obstacles and setbacks.
- **Patience:** Be patient with your family members, especially when they are struggling or facing challenges. Give them the time and space they need to grow and learn at their own pace.
- **Compassion:** Show empathy and understanding towards your family members, and strive to see things from their perspective. Offer a listening ear and a helping hand when they are in need.
- **Trust:** Build trust within your family by being reliable, consistent, and honest in your words and actions. Create a safe and supportive environment where everyone feels secure and loved.

Prayer:

Heavenly Father, thank You for the gift of unconditional love that You have shown us through Your Son, Jesus Christ. Help us to practice this love within our families, accepting and cherishing each member for who they are. Teach us to forgive, encourage, and support one another as we grow and learn together.

Grant us the patience, compassion, and trust needed to nurture strong and loving relationships within our family. May our home be a place of love, safety, and unity, where everyone feels valued and accepted.

In Jesus' name, we pray. Amen.

Lord Teach Me To

I Am Thankful For

Action Step:

This week, make an effort to practice unconditional love with each member of your family.

Offer acceptance, forgiveness, encouragement, patience, and trust.

Pray for God's guidance in helping you create a loving and supportive family environment where everyone feels valued and cherished.

Day 25: Fostering a Spirit of Gratitude

Scripture:

"Give thanks in all circumstances; for this is God's will for you in Christ Jesus." - 1 Thessalonians 5:18 (NIV)

Reflection:

Gratitude is a powerful practice that can bring a wealth of benefits to both individuals and families. When we cultivate a spirit of gratitude within our family, we are nurturing an attitude of appreciation and thankfulness for the many blessings that fill our lives. Gratitude can help shift our focus from what we lack to what we have, fostering contentment and happiness.

Here are some ways to foster a spirit of gratitude within your family:

- **Daily Gratitude Practice:** Encourage each family member to share something they are grateful for each day. This can be done during dinner, bedtime, or any other time when the family is gathered together.

- **Gratitude Journal:** Provide each family member with a gratitude journal where they can write down their daily blessings. Encourage them to write at least three things they are grateful for each day.

- **Acts of Kindness:** Encourage family members to show their appreciation for each other by performing acts of kindness. This can be as simple as a warm hug, a loving note, or a surprise treat.

- **Thankful Prayers:** Include expressions of gratitude in your family prayers. Encourage family members to thank God for specific blessings in their lives.

- **Gratitude Reminders:** Display quotes, Bible verses, or artwork around your home that remind your family to be grateful. These visual cues can serve as daily reminders to appreciate the abundance in our lives.

Prayer:

Heavenly Father, we thank You for the many blessings You bestow upon our family each day. Help us to cultivate a spirit of gratitude within our home, recognizing and appreciating the abundant gifts that surround us.

Teach us to be thankful in all circumstances, and to show our appreciation for each other through acts of kindness and love.

May our family become a beacon of gratitude, shining Your light and love into the world.

In Jesus' name, we pray. Amen.

Lord Teach Me To

I Am Thankful For

Action Step:

This week, implement one or more of the suggested practices to foster a spirit of gratitude within your family.

Encourage each family member to participate, and notice the positive impact that gratitude can have on your family's overall well-being and happiness.

Day 26: Teaching Responsibility and Accountability

Scripture:

"Train up a child in the way he should go; even when he is old he will not depart from it." - Proverbs 22:6 (ESV)

Reflection:

One of the most important lessons we can teach our children is the value of responsibility and accountability. When children learn to take responsibility for their actions and to be accountable for their mistakes, they develop a strong foundation of character that will serve them well throughout their lives.

Here are some ways to teach responsibility and accountability within your family:

- Lead by example: Model responsibility and accountability in your own life. Show your children that you take responsibility for your actions and own up to your mistakes.

- Assign age-appropriate chores: Give your children chores that are appropriate for their age and abilities. This helps them learn responsibility and the importance of contributing to the family.

- Encourage problem-solving: When your children encounter difficulties or make mistakes, guide them in finding solutions and learning from their experiences.

- Set expectations and consequences: Establish clear expectations for your children's behavior and outline the consequences for not meeting those expectations. Be consistent in enforcing these consequences when necessary.

- Praise responsible behavior: Acknowledge and praise your children when they demonstrate responsibility and accountability. This will reinforce the importance of these values and encourage them to continue making responsible choices.

Prayer:

Dear Lord, we ask for Your guidance in teaching our children the importance of responsibility and accountability. Help us to lead by example and to provide them with the tools they need to develop strong character.

Grant us wisdom and patience as we guide our children in making responsible choices and learning from their mistakes.

May our family be a shining example of integrity, responsibility, and accountability, reflecting Your love and guidance.

In Jesus' name, we pray. Amen.

Lord Teach Me To

I Am Thankful For

Action Step:

This week, focus on teaching responsibility and accountability within your family. Implement one or more of the suggested practices and have open discussions about the importance of these values.

Observe the positive impact these lessons have on your children's behavior and overall character development.

Day 27: Growing Together through Life Transitions

Scripture:

"Trust in the LORD with all your heart, and do not lean on your own understanding. In all your ways acknowledge him, and he will make straight your paths." - Proverbs 3:5-6 (ESV)

Reflection:

Life is full of transitions – births, graduations, marriages, career changes, and loss. Each of these events brings new challenges and opportunities for growth within the family. Navigating these transitions can be difficult, but by relying on our faith and staying committed to one another, we can grow closer together as a family.

Here are some tips for growing together through life transitions:

- **Acknowledge the change:** Recognize the significance of the transition and its impact on your family. Allow space for emotions and discussions about the change.

- **Communicate openly:** Keep the lines of communication open within the family. Share your feelings, thoughts, and concerns with one another, and listen empathetically to each family member's perspective.

- **Be flexible and adaptable:** Embrace the need to adjust your family's routines, roles, and responsibilities during transitions. Remain open to change and be willing to make necessary adjustments.

- **Offer support and encouragement:** Be there for one another during these challenging times. Offer emotional support, encouragement, and practical help as needed.

- **Rely on your faith:** Turn to God for guidance, strength, and comfort during times of transition. Pray together as a family, seek God's wisdom, and trust in His plan for your lives.

Prayer:

Heavenly Father, we thank You for the many blessings and experiences You have provided for our family. As we face life's transitions, we ask for Your guidance, wisdom, and strength.

Help us to grow closer together as a family during these times, relying on Your love and faithfulness.

Grant us the ability to communicate openly, to be flexible and adaptable, and to support one another through the challenges we face.

In Jesus' name, we pray. Amen.

Lord Teach Me To

I Am Thankful For

Action Step:

This week, discuss any upcoming or recent life transitions within your family.

Encourage open communication, share your feelings, and support one another.

Pray together, asking for God's guidance and wisdom during these times of change.

Day 28: Strengthening Family Bonds through Humor

Scripture:

"A joyful heart is good medicine, but a crushed spirit dries up the bones."
- Proverbs 17:22 (ESV)

Reflection:

Laughter and humor can bring joy and healing to the heart, helping to lighten the mood and relieve stress within the family. Sharing jokes, funny stories, and amusing experiences can create a warm, loving atmosphere and foster a sense of unity and belonging. Moreover, laughter promotes emotional and mental well-being, making it an essential element in nurturing strong family bonds.

Here are some ideas for incorporating humor into your family life:

- **Share funny stories:** Set aside time during family gatherings, mealtimes, or before bedtime to share amusing anecdotes from your day or recall humorous experiences from the past.

- **Encourage creativity:** Provide opportunities for family members to express their humor through creative outlets, such as writing jokes, drawing cartoons, or performing skits.

- **Watch or attend comedy shows:** Enjoy family-friendly comedy movies, TV shows, or live performances together. This can provide a shared experience and offer conversation starters about the humor you enjoyed.

- **Play games:** Engage in fun, lighthearted games that encourage laughter, such as charades, Pictionary, or other humorous group activities.

- **Be silly:** Don't be afraid to let your guard down and be playful with your family members. Sing silly songs, engage in spontaneous dance parties, or make funny faces — whatever brings a smile to everyone's faces.

Prayer:

Dear Lord, thank You for the gift of laughter and the joy it brings to our hearts.

We ask for Your help in incorporating humor into our family life and for the wisdom to recognize when laughter is needed.

Guide us as we share funny stories, play games, and enjoy comedy together, strengthening our family bonds through humor.

Let our joyful hearts be a reflection of Your love and grace in our lives.

In Jesus' name, we pray. Amen.

Lord Teach Me To

I Am Thankful For

Action Step:

This week, make an effort to bring more laughter and humor into your family life.

Share funny stories, engage in lighthearted games, and enjoy comedy together. Reflect on the positive impact that laughter has on your family relationships and emotional well-being.

Day 29: The Importance of Family Support Networks

Scripture:

"Two are better than one, because they have a good return for their labor: If either of them falls down, one can help the other up. But pity anyone who falls and has no one to help them up."
 - Ecclesiastes 4:9-10 (NIV)

Reflection:

Every family encounters challenges and hardships, making it crucial to have a strong support network. A reliable support system provides encouragement, advice, and a sense of belonging, helping family members navigate the ups and downs of life. Building and maintaining strong relationships within and outside the family unit can offer a wealth of emotional, practical, and spiritual support.

Here are some ways to cultivate a solid family support network:

- **Nurture relationships with extended family:** Stay connected with grandparents, aunts, uncles, and cousins through regular phone calls, visits, and family gatherings. These relationships can provide a valuable source of love, wisdom, and guidance.
- **Connect with other families:** Build friendships with other families who share similar values, interests, and beliefs. Participate in community events, join parenting groups, or attend faith-based activities to meet like-minded individuals.
- **Seek professional support:** When necessary, reach out to professionals, such as therapists, counselors, or social workers, for expert guidance in addressing specific family issues or challenges.
- **Engage in spiritual communities:** Get involved in your local faith community by attending worship services, joining small groups, or participating in outreach programs. This can provide a supportive environment for spiritual growth and encouragement.
- **Foster open communication:** Encourage honest and open communication within your family. By discussing challenges and seeking support from one another, you create a safe space for mutual understanding and assistance.

Prayer:

Heavenly Father, we thank You for the gift of family and the support networks we can build together. Help us to nurture relationships within our extended family, connect with other families, and engage in our spiritual communities to strengthen our support system.

Guide us as we seek professional help when needed, and teach us to foster open communication within our family.

May we always be there for each other, offering love, encouragement, and guidance in times of need.

In Jesus' name, we pray. Amen.

Lord Teach Me To	**I Am Thankful For**

Action Step:

This week, take steps to strengthen your family support network.

Reach out to extended family members, connect with other families, or get involved in community or faith-based activities. Reflect on the ways these connections positively impact your family's well-being and resilience.

Day 30: Encouraging Openness and Honesty

Scripture:

"Therefore each of you must put off falsehood and speak truthfully to your neighbor, for we are all members of one body."
- Ephesians 4:25 (NIV)

Reflection:

Openness and honesty are crucial components of healthy family relationships. Fostering an environment where family members feel comfortable sharing their thoughts and feelings promotes trust, understanding, and emotional intimacy. By encouraging open communication, family members can resolve conflicts, express love and appreciation, and better understand one another's needs and perspectives.

Here are some strategies to encourage openness and honesty within your family:

- **Create a safe space:** Ensure that your home is a place where family members feel safe and comfortable expressing their emotions, opinions, and concerns. Be respectful, empathetic, and non-judgmental when listening to others.
- **Model honesty:** Set an example by being truthful, open, and genuine in your interactions with family members. When you are honest about your feelings, thoughts, and experiences, you create an environment where others feel comfortable doing the same.
- **Encourage expression:** Encourage family members to express their emotions and thoughts openly, without fear of judgment or criticism. Provide opportunities for each person to share their perspectives and feelings during family discussions or one-on-one conversations.
- **Validate emotions:** Validate and acknowledge the feelings of your family members, even if you don't necessarily agree with them. This demonstrates that their emotions are important and that you care about their well-being.
- **Practice active listening:** When a family member is sharing their thoughts or feelings, listen attentively and respond with empathy and understanding. Give your full attention and avoid interrupting or offering unsolicited advice.

Prayer:

Heavenly Father, we thank You for the gift of open and honest communication within our family. Help us to create a safe and loving environment where each family member feels comfortable sharing their thoughts, feelings, and experiences.

Guide us in modeling honesty, encouraging expression, validating emotions, and practicing active listening.

May our family grow stronger and more united through our commitment to open communication and understanding.

In Jesus' name, we pray. Amen.

Lord Teach Me To	I Am Thankful For

Action Step:

This week, focus on creating opportunities for open and honest communication within your family.

Share your feelings and experiences, encourage others to do the same, and practice active listening.

Reflect on the positive impact these efforts have on your family's relationships and overall well-being.

Day 31: The Role of Discipline in Family Life

Scripture:

"My son, do not despise the Lord's discipline, and do not resent his rebuke, because the Lord disciplines those he loves, as a father the son he delights in." - Proverbs 3:11-12 (NIV)

Reflection:

Discipline is an essential aspect of family life. It helps to establish order, teach responsibility, and promote personal growth. As parents, it is crucial to provide guidance and boundaries while also demonstrating love and compassion. The goal of discipline is not to punish but to help children learn from their mistakes and develop the skills and values necessary to thrive in life.

Here are some principles to consider when disciplining your children:

- **Consistency:** Be consistent in enforcing rules and consequences. Inconsistency can lead to confusion, resentment, and lack of respect for authority.
- **Fairness:** Ensure that the consequences are appropriate and proportional to the offense. Unfair punishment can damage your relationship with your child and hinder their emotional development.
- **Communication:** Explain the reasons behind the rules and the consequences of breaking them. Help your child understand the importance of adhering to these guidelines and the potential impact of their actions on themselves and others.
- **Positive reinforcement:** Praise and reward good behavior to encourage its continuation. Acknowledging and celebrating positive actions can be more effective than focusing solely on negative behavior.
- **Teach by example:** Model the values and behaviors you wish to see in your children. They are more likely to adopt these principles when they see them consistently demonstrated by their parents.
- **Focus on the behavior, not the child:** When correcting your child, address the specific behavior that needs to change, rather than labeling or criticizing the child as a person. This helps them understand that they can improve and grow.

Prayer:

Heavenly Father, thank You for Your loving discipline and guidance in our lives. Help us to apply the principles of discipline in our family life with wisdom, fairness, and compassion.

Grant us the strength and patience to be consistent, communicate effectively, and model the values we wish our children to embrace.

May our discipline be rooted in love and aimed at nurturing their growth and development.

In Jesus' name, we pray. Amen.

Lord Teach Me To	I Am Thankful For

Action Step:

Reflect on your approach to discipline within your family.

Consider the principles discussed above and identify areas where you can improve or adjust your methods.

Commit to implementing these changes and observe the impact on your family's dynamics and relationships.

Day 32: The Power of Family Prayer and Worship

Scripture:

"But as for me and my household, we will serve the Lord."
- Joshua 24:15 (NIV)

Reflection:

The power of family prayer and worship cannot be overstated. When families come together to pray and worship, they create a strong spiritual foundation that nurtures love, unity, and faith. By dedicating time to seek God's presence together, families can foster a deep, enduring relationship with Him and experience His love and guidance in their lives.

Here are some benefits of incorporating prayer and worship into your family life:

- **Strengthening bonds:** Shared spiritual experiences can create stronger emotional connections and help family members feel more united and supported.

- **Establishing values:** Praying and worshiping together helps reinforce the importance of faith and spiritual values in daily life, providing a strong moral compass for children as they grow and develop.

- **Encouraging spiritual growth:** Regular family prayer and worship allows each family member to deepen their relationship with God and develop a personal faith that can sustain them through life's challenges.

- **Inviting God's presence:** When families invite God into their home through prayer and worship, they create an atmosphere of peace, love, and joy that can transform their relationships and daily experiences.

- **Developing resilience:** Praying and worshiping together can help families navigate difficult times, providing strength and hope to face life's challenges.

Prayer:

Heavenly Father, thank You for the gift of family and the opportunity to grow together in faith. We ask You to bless our family as we commit to praying and worshiping together.

Help us to create a strong spiritual foundation that nurtures love, unity, and a deep relationship with You.

May our home be filled with Your presence, and may our family be a light in this world, reflecting Your love and grace.

In Jesus' name, we pray. Amen.

Lord Teach Me To	**I Am Thankful For**

Action Step:

If you haven't already, establish a regular family prayer and worship routine.

Choose a time, place, and format that works best for your family, and commit to consistently seeking God's presence together.

Observe the positive impact this practice has on your family's relationships and spiritual growth.

Day 33: Developing Resilience as a Family

Scripture:

"We are hard pressed on every side, but not crushed; perplexed, but not in despair; persecuted, but not abandoned; struck down, but not destroyed."
- 2 Corinthians 4:8-9 (NIV)

Reflection:

Life is filled with challenges and hardships that can test the strength and unity of a family. Resilience is the ability to adapt and thrive in the face of adversity, and it plays a crucial role in maintaining a strong and healthy family dynamic. Developing resilience as a family can help you navigate difficult times with hope, courage, and strength.

Here are some practical ways to build resilience as a family:

- **Cultivate a strong support system:** Building a network of friends, relatives, and community members who can offer help, encouragement, and understanding during challenging times can help families feel supported and better equipped to face adversity.
- **Maintain open communication:** Encourage family members to share their thoughts, feelings, and concerns openly and honestly. This fosters a safe and supportive environment in which everyone can express themselves and seek comfort.
- **Teach problem-solving skills:** Equip your family members with the ability to identify and address challenges and conflicts constructively. By developing problem-solving skills, you can help your family members gain confidence in their ability to overcome obstacles.
- **Foster a positive attitude:** Encourage an optimistic outlook and help family members focus on the positive aspects of their lives. By practicing gratitude and focusing on the blessings in your lives, your family can cultivate a hopeful perspective in the face of adversity.
- **Prioritize self-care:** Encourage family members to take care of their physical, mental, and emotional well-being. Healthy habits, such as regular exercise, balanced nutrition, and sufficient rest, can provide the foundation for resilience and well-being.

Prayer:

Dear Lord, thank You for the gift of family and the strength we find in each other. We pray for Your guidance as we work together to develop resilience in the face of life's challenges.

Help us to cultivate open communication, support one another, and rely on our faith to navigate difficult times.

May our family grow stronger and more united through adversity, and may we always trust in Your unfailing love and protection.

In Jesus' name, we pray. Amen.

Lord Teach Me To

I Am Thankful For

Action Step:

Identify an area in which your family can work together to develop greater resilience.

This may be improving communication, strengthening your support system, or fostering a positive attitude.

Commit to taking intentional steps to build resilience in this area and observe the impact on your family's ability to navigate challenges.

Day 34: Cultivating a Heart of Generosity

Scripture:

"Give, and it will be given to you. A good measure, pressed down, shaken together and running over, will be poured into your lap. For with the measure you use, it will be measured to you." - Luke 6:38 (NIV)

Reflection:

Generosity is a powerful force that has the ability to strengthen family bonds and create a positive impact on the world around us. Cultivating a heart of generosity within your family not only enriches the lives of others but also fosters personal growth.
Here are some practical ways to encourage generosity in your family:

- **Model generosity:** As parents and caregivers, you have the unique opportunity to set an example for your children by demonstrating acts of generosity in your daily life. Share your time, talents, and resources with others, and discuss the impact of your actions with your family.
- **Teach empathy and compassion:** Help your family members develop an understanding of the needs and feelings of others. Encourage them to put themselves in other people's shoes and consider how they can make a positive difference in someone's life.
- **Involve the whole family:** Make generosity a family affair by engaging in acts of service and giving together. Volunteer at a local organization, participate in a charity event, or create a family giving fund to support causes that are meaningful to your family.
- **Encourage acts of kindness:** Encourage family members to perform random acts of kindness for friends, neighbors, and even strangers. These small gestures can create a ripple effect of kindness and generosity that extends far beyond your family.
- **Reflect on the blessings in your life:** Regularly discuss the gifts and blessings in your family's life, and express gratitude for all that you have. This practice can help cultivate a mindset of abundance and generosity.
- **Set realistic expectations:** Teach your family members the importance of balancing their own needs with the needs of others. Encourage them to give generously, but also to be mindful of their own well-being and personal limits.

Prayer:

Heavenly Father, we thank You for the abundant blessings in our lives and for the opportunity to share Your love and generosity with others. Help us to cultivate a heart of generosity within our family, and guide us in our efforts to serve and support those in need.

May our family be a shining example of Your love and compassion in the world. Help us to be mindful of the needs of others and to give freely, with open hearts and open hands.

In Jesus' name, we pray. Amen.

Lord Teach Me To	I Am Thankful For

Action Step:

Identify a specific act of generosity or service that your family can participate in together.

Discuss the importance of generosity and the impact it can have on the lives of others.

After completing the act of generosity, reflect on the experience as a family and discuss how it felt to give and serve others.

Scripture:

"Though one may be overpowered, two can defend themselves. A cord of three strands is not quickly broken." - Ecclesiastes 4:12 (NIV)

Reflection:

A strong and healthy marriage or partnership lays the foundation for a stable and nurturing family environment. To strengthen your relationship with your spouse or partner, it is essential to invest time, effort, and love into your partnership. Fostering open communication, mutual respect, and emotional support will create a solid foundation for your family life.

Here are some ways to strengthen your marriage or partnership:

- **Prioritize quality time together:** In the midst of busy schedules, it is important to make time for one another. Schedule regular date nights, and make an effort to engage in meaningful conversation and shared activities.
- **Practice open communication:** Encourage honest and open communication with your spouse or partner. Share your thoughts, feelings, and concerns with one another, and listen attentively and empathetically.
- **Show appreciation and gratitude:** Express gratitude and appreciation for your spouse or partner regularly. Offer compliments, express love, and acknowledge the positive qualities and actions of your partner.
- **Support one another:** Offer emotional support and encouragement during challenging times, and celebrate achievements and milestones together. Be each other's biggest cheerleader and advocate.
- **Resolve conflicts with love and respect:** Disagreements are a natural part of any relationship. Approach conflicts with understanding, empathy, and respect, and work together to find solutions that benefit both partners.
- **Nurture your spiritual connection:** Share your spiritual beliefs, practices, and experiences with your spouse or partner. Pray and worship together, and engage in spiritual activities that bring you closer to one another and to God.

Prayer:

Dear Lord, we thank You for the gift of marriage and partnership. We ask for Your guidance and wisdom as we strive to strengthen our relationship and create a loving and supportive environment for our family.

Help us to prioritize quality time together, practice open communication, and show appreciation and gratitude for one another. Teach us to resolve conflicts with love and respect, and to nurture our spiritual connection with You and each other.

We pray for Your continued blessings upon our marriage or partnership and our family as a whole. In Jesus' name, we pray. Amen.

Lord Teach Me To	I Am Thankful For

Action Step:

Plan a special date night or activity with your spouse or partner this week, focusing on spending quality time together and nurturing your emotional connection.

Discuss your relationship goals and how you can work together to achieve them in order to strengthen your partnership.

Scripture:

"Start children off on the way they should go, and even when they are old they will not turn from it." - Proverbs 22:6 (NIV)

Reflection:

As parents and caregivers, one of our most important responsibilities is guiding our children through their spiritual formation. By nurturing their spiritual development, we can help them establish a strong foundation of faith that will sustain them throughout their lives.

Here are some ways to guide your children through spiritual formation:

- **Model a strong faith:** Children learn from observing the adults around them. Be intentional about living out your faith and demonstrating your values through your actions, words, and decisions.
- **Create a spiritual atmosphere at home:** Encourage an environment where faith is nurtured through prayer, Bible reading, and discussions about spiritual matters. Make time for family devotionals and worship together.
- **Involve your children in spiritual activities:** Include your children in church activities, Sunday school, and youth groups where they can develop relationships with other believers and grow in their faith.
- **Teach your children about the Bible:** Read Bible stories together and discuss the lessons they can learn from the characters and events. Encourage them to ask questions and share their thoughts.
- **Pray with and for your children:** Pray together as a family and teach your children to pray individually. Let them know you are praying for them and their spiritual growth.
- **Encourage them to serve others:** Involve your children in acts of service and kindness to others, both within your family and in your community. This will help them develop a heart for others and grow in their faith.
- **Celebrate milestones and rituals:** Mark significant moments in your children's spiritual journey, such as baptism, confirmation, or first communion, by creating meaningful family traditions and rituals.

Prayer:

Heavenly Father, thank You for the gift of our children and the opportunity to guide them in their spiritual formation.

Help us to be effective role models of faith and to create a nurturing environment for their spiritual growth. Grant us wisdom, patience, and love as we support them on their journey. In Jesus' name, Amen.

Lord Teach Me To	I Am Thankful For

Action Step:

Reflect on your own spiritual journey and consider what practices have been most impactful in your personal growth. Identify areas where you can model strong faith for your children.

Set aside a specific time each day or week for family devotionals or worship. Keep this time consistent and prioritize it in your family's schedule.

Look for age-appropriate spiritual activities and opportunities for your children, such as Sunday school, youth groups, or Bible camps. Encourage their involvement and make an effort to support them in these activities.

Remember, as you guide your children through their spiritual formation, be patient, supportive, and loving. Celebrate their progress and continue to nurture their faith as they grow.

Day 37: Embracing the Legacy of Family

Scripture:

"Children's children are a crown to the aged, and parents are the pride of their children." - Proverbs 17:6 (NIV)

Reflection:

Family is more than just those who share our bloodline; it is a rich tapestry woven from the experiences, stories, and wisdom of generations before us. Embracing the legacy of our family means understanding and appreciating our roots, preserving the traditions and values of our ancestors, and passing them on to future generations.

Here are some ways to embrace the legacy of your family:
- **Explore your family history:** Delve into your family's past by researching genealogy, interviewing older relatives, and gathering photographs, letters, and artifacts that tell your family's story. Share your findings with your children to help them understand their heritage and roots.
- **Preserve family traditions:** Identify meaningful traditions and rituals from your family's past and incorporate them into your family's present. These may include special meals, holiday customs, or religious observances that have been passed down through the generations.
- **Learn from your family's wisdom:** Listen to the stories, advice, and experiences of your elders, and absorb the lessons they have learned throughout their lives. Encourage your children to engage with their grandparents and other older relatives to gain valuable insights and wisdom.
- **Honor your family's values:** Reflect on the values and principles that have shaped your family's identity and made it what it is today. Strive to **live out those values and pass them on to your children.**
- **Create your own family legacy:** As you embrace the legacy of your family, consider what unique contributions you can make to your family's story. What traditions, values, and wisdom do you want to pass on to future generations? Be intentional about creating a lasting legacy for your children and grandchildren to cherish.

Prayer:

Lord, thank You for the rich legacy of our family and the wisdom, experiences, and traditions that have been passed down through the generations. Help us to embrace our family's heritage, learn from the past, and create a lasting legacy for our children and grandchildren.

Guide us as we strive to live out our family's values and pass them on to future generations. In Jesus' name, Amen.

Lord Teach Me To

I Am Thankful For

Action Step:

Spend time reflecting on your family's history, traditions, and values. Make a list of the aspects of your family's legacy that you want to preserve and pass on to future generations.

Plan a family activity, such as a special meal or a visit to a place of significance to your family's history, to celebrate and honor your family's heritage.

Reach out to older relatives and ask them to share their stories, memories, and wisdom. Record their responses in a journal or make an audio or video recording to preserve their memories for future generations.

Reflect on the values and principles that have shaped your family's identity. Make a commitment to live out these values and pass them on to your children through your words, actions, and example.

Scripture:

"Above all, love each other deeply, because love covers over a multitude of sins. Offer hospitality to one another without grumbling."
- 1 Peter 4:8-9 (NIV)

Reflection:

In today's fast-paced world, it's easy for families to become disconnected from their extended family members. However, maintaining strong connections with grandparents, aunts, uncles, and cousins can provide a valuable support network and enrich our lives. By nurturing these relationships, we can create a sense of belonging and unity within our family.

Here are some ways to build a stronger connection with your extended family:
- **Make an effort to stay in touch:** With modern technology, staying connected has never been easier. Schedule regular video calls, send emails, or use social media to keep in touch with your extended family members.
- **Plan family gatherings:** Organize family reunions, holiday celebrations, or informal get-togethers to bring everyone together. Use these occasions to create memories, strengthen bonds, and celebrate your family's unique culture and traditions.
- **Show interest in their lives:** Take the time to learn about your relatives' interests, hobbies, and experiences. Ask questions and listen actively to their stories, which will help you develop a deeper understanding and appreciation of each other.
- **Offer support and encouragement:** Be there for your extended family members in times of need. Offer a listening ear, provide practical help, or simply let them know you care.
- **Celebrate milestones together:** Acknowledge and celebrate the accomplishments, milestones, and special events in your relatives' lives. Send cards, make phone calls, or plan visits to share in their joy.
- **Practice forgiveness and grace:** Like any relationship, there may be conflicts and misunderstandings within the extended family. Be willing to forgive, extend grace, and seek reconciliation when needed.

Prayer:

Lord, thank You for the gift of our extended family. Help us to cultivate strong connections and nurture these relationships.

Give us the wisdom, patience, and love needed to foster unity and support within our family. In Jesus' name, Amen.

Lord Teach Me To	I Am Thankful For

Action Step:

Make a list of your extended family members with whom you'd like to build stronger connections.

Choose one or two specific ways to reach out and connect with each person on your list. This could include scheduling a regular video call, sending a thoughtful message, or planning a visit.

Set aside time in your schedule to intentionally focus on building these relationships. Remember, nurturing connections with your extended family takes effort and commitment.

Encourage your children to develop relationships with their extended family members as well. Share family stories and involve them in the process of connecting with their relatives.

Reflect on the progress you've made in building stronger connections with your extended family and make adjustments as needed to continue fostering these important relationships.

Day 39: The Impact of Family on Personal Growth

Scripture:

"As iron sharpens iron, so one person sharpens another."
- Proverbs 27:17 (NIV)

Reflection:

Our family plays a significant role in shaping our personal growth and development. The relationships we have with our parents, siblings, and other family members influence our values, beliefs, and attitudes towards life. Family experiences can serve as a catalyst for personal growth, helping us become the best version of ourselves.

Here are some ways your family can impact your personal growth:

- **Emotional support:** A supportive family environment can provide a safe space to express emotions and share experiences. This emotional support can help us navigate life's challenges with greater resilience and confidence.
- **Learning from each other:** Family members offer diverse perspectives, experiences, and knowledge, providing opportunities for learning and growth. Engaging in open and honest conversations can help us expand our understanding of the world and ourselves.
- **Providing guidance and advice:** Our family members can serve as mentors and role models, offering valuable guidance and advice based on their own experiences. This guidance can help us make better decisions and chart our own unique paths in life.
- **Encouraging personal development:** A loving and supportive family can encourage us to pursue our passions, interests, and goals. They can provide us with the motivation and resources needed to grow and achieve our full potential.
- **Holding us accountable:** Healthy family relationships can help keep us accountable for our actions and choices. This accountability can drive us to make positive changes in our lives and strive for continuous self-improvement.

Prayer:

Dear Lord, thank You for the gift of family and the many ways they contribute to our personal growth. Help us to nurture and strengthen our family bonds, creating a supportive environment where each member can grow and flourish. Teach us to value the wisdom and experiences of our loved ones and to learn from one another. In Jesus' name, Amen.

Lord Teach Me To

I Am Thankful For

Action Step:

Reflect on the ways your family has contributed to your personal growth. Take a moment to appreciate the impact they have had on your life and development.

Initiate a conversation with your family members about personal growth. Share your thoughts on how you have grown together and the lessons you have learned from one another.

Make a commitment to hold each other accountable for personal growth and self-improvement. Establish a regular check-in or family meeting to discuss progress, challenges, and ways to support one another in achieving your goals.

Remember, nurturing your family relationships and fostering personal growth is an ongoing process. Keep the lines of communication open and continue to support one another as you grow together.

Day 40: Celebrating the Journey of Family Life

Scripture:

"I will be your God throughout your lifetime—until your hair is white with age. I made you, and I will care for you. I will carry you along and save you." - Isaiah 46:4 (NLT)

Reflection:

Family life is a beautiful journey filled with moments of joy, laughter, growth, and connection. As you have traveled through these 40 days, you have likely experienced both challenges and victories in your efforts to strengthen your family bonds. It's important to take the time to celebrate your progress and express gratitude for the gift of family.

Here are some ideas for celebrating the journey of family life:
- **Share your gratitude:** Gather your family and express your appreciation for the love, support, and growth you have experienced together. Encourage each family member to share their thoughts and feelings as well.
- **Create a family memory book:** Compile a collection of photographs, letters, artwork, and other mementos that represent the memories and experiences you have shared as a family. This will serve as a cherished keepsake to look back on in the years to come.
- **Establish a family tradition:** Create a unique family tradition that honors your journey together. This could be an annual celebration, a special meal, or a memorable activity that brings everyone together.
- **Reflect on your growth:** As a family, discuss the growth and progress you have made throughout the 40 days. Acknowledge the challenges you have faced, the lessons you have learned, and the ways you have grown closer.
- **Plan for the future:** Together, discuss your hopes and dreams for your family's future. Set goals and create a vision for how you will continue to grow and support one another in the coming months and years.

As you celebrate the journey of family life, remember that the love, support, and connection you share are the most valuable gifts you can give to one another. Cherish each moment and continue to nurture the bonds that hold you together.

Prayer:

Heavenly Father, thank You for the incredible journey of family life.
We are grateful for the love, connection, and growth we have experienced
together. Help us to continue to support and encourage one another as we face
the challenges and joys that lie ahead.
May we always remember the gift of family and celebrate the journey we share.
In Jesus' name, Amen.

Lord Teach Me To

I Am Thankful For

Action Step:

Plan a family celebration: Organize a special event or gathering to honor
and celebrate your family's journey together. This can be a simple dinner,
a picnic, or a day of fun activities that everyone can enjoy.

Share appreciation: During the celebration, encourage each family
member to express their appreciation for one another and share a specific
memory or moment that brought them closer together.

Set future goals: As a family, discuss your hopes, dreams, and goals for
the future. Create a shared vision of how you will continue to grow and
strengthen your family bonds.

Commit to ongoing growth: Make a commitment as a family to continue
nurturing your relationships and growing together. Establish regular
check-ins or family meetings to discuss your progress and address any
challenges that arise.

Week 1: Building a Strong Foundation

Weekly Reflection

Look back on the first week of daily devotionals and consider the role that faith plays in the foundation of your family.

What steps have you taken to strengthen that foundation?

Discuss any new insights or changes you've experienced as a family.

Journal Prompt

Write about your family's spiritual foundation and the areas where you would like to see growth or improvement.

Week 2: Enhancing Communication and Connection

Weekly Reflection

Reflect on the ways your family communicates with one another.
In what areas can you improve?

What new communication strategies have you tried?

Share your thoughts and experiences with your family.

Journal Prompt

Describe any changes you've noticed in your family's communication patterns and the impact they've had on your relationships.

Week 3: Creating a Supportive Home Environment

Weekly Reflection

Consider the atmosphere of your home and how it impacts your family's relationships.

What steps have you taken to create a supportive environment?

Share any positive changes or challenges that have arisen.

Journal Prompt

Write about the ways you've made your home more supportive and nurturing for your family.

Weekly Reflection

Reflect on the family rituals and traditions you've established or strengthened during this journey.

How have they brought your family closer together?

Discuss your favorite rituals and the significance they hold.

Journal Prompt

Write about the traditions and rituals your family has embraced, and the impact they've had on your relationships.

Week 5: Encouraging Emotional and Spiritual Growth

Weekly Reflection

Consider the ways you've nurtured emotional and spiritual growth in your family members.

What new strategies have you implemented?

Share any insights, challenges, or growth you've experienced.

Journal Prompt

Describe how you've supported your family's emotional and spiritual development and the changes you've observed in their well-being.

Week 6: Overcoming Challenges and Growing Together

Weekly Reflection

Reflect on the challenges your family has faced during this journey and how you've worked together to overcome them.

What lessons have you learned, and how have you grown as a family?

Journal Prompt

Write about the challenges your family has faced and the ways in which
you've come together to support one another.

Week 7: Building a Legacy of Love and Unity

Weekly Reflection

Look back on your journey and consider the legacy of love and unity you're creating for your family.

What steps have you taken to strengthen your family bonds?

Share your thoughts, experiences, and the vision you have for your family's future.

Journal Prompt

Write about the legacy you wish to leave for your family and the steps you're taking to create a lasting bond of love and unity.

Day : _____

Reflection

_____
_____
_____
_____
_____
_____
_____
_____
_____

Bible Passage : _____

_____
_____
_____
_____
_____
_____
_____
_____
_____
_____
_____
_____
_____
_____
_____
_____

Application

Lord Teach Me To

I Am Thankful For

Prayer

Day : _____

Reflection

_____
_____
_____
_____
_____
_____
_____
_____

Bible Passage : _____

_____
_____
_____
_____
_____
_____
_____
_____
_____
_____
_____
_____
_____
_____
_____

Application

Lord Teach Me To

I Am Thankful For

Prayer

Day : _____

Reflection

_____
_____
_____
_____
_____
_____
_____
_____
_____

Bible Passage : _____

_____
_____
_____
_____
_____
_____
_____
_____
_____
_____
_____
_____
_____
_____
_____
_____
_____

Application

Lord Teach Me To

I Am Thankful For

Prayer

Day : _____

Reflection

_____
_____
_____
_____
_____
_____
_____
_____
_____

Bible Passage : _____

_____
_____
_____
_____
_____
_____
_____
_____
_____
_____
_____
_____
_____
_____
_____
_____

Application

Lord Teach Me To

I Am Thankful For

Prayer

Day : _____

Reflection

_____
_____
_____
_____
_____
_____
_____
_____

Bible Passage : _____

_____
_____
_____
_____
_____
_____
_____
_____
_____
_____
_____
_____
_____
_____
_____

Application

Lord Teach Me To

I Am Thankful For

Prayer

Day : _____

Reflection

_____
_____
_____
_____
_____
_____
_____
_____

Bible Passage : _____

_____
_____
_____
_____
_____
_____
_____
_____
_____
_____
_____
_____
_____
_____
_____
_____

Application

Lord Teach Me To

I Am Thankful For

Prayer

Day : _____

Reflection

_____
_____
_____
_____
_____
_____
_____
_____

Bible Passage : _____

_____
_____
_____
_____
_____
_____
_____
_____
_____
_____
_____
_____
_____
_____
_____
_____

Application

_____
_____
_____
_____
_____

Lord Teach Me To

I Am Thankful For

Prayer

Day : _____

Reflection

_____
_____
_____
_____
_____
_____
_____
_____
_____

Bible Passage : _____

_____
_____
_____
_____
_____
_____
_____
_____
_____
_____
_____
_____
_____
_____
_____
_____

Application

_____
_____
_____
_____
_____

Lord Teach Me To	I Am Thankful For

Prayer

_____
_____
_____
_____

Day : _____

Reflection

_____
_____
_____
_____
_____
_____
_____
_____

Bible Passage : _____

_____
_____
_____
_____
_____
_____
_____
_____
_____
_____
_____
_____
_____
_____
_____
_____

Application

Lord Teach Me To

I Am Thankful For

Prayer

Day : _____

Reflection

_____
_____
_____
_____
_____
_____
_____
_____

Bible Passage : _____

_____
_____
_____
_____
_____
_____
_____
_____
_____
_____
_____
_____
_____
_____
_____
_____
_____

Application

Lord Teach Me To

I Am Thankful For

Prayer

Conclusion

As we come to the conclusion of this **40-day journey**, take a moment to reflect on the incredible strides you've made in strengthening your family bonds. The devotionals, prayers, and action steps you've engaged in have provided valuable tools to help you build a more loving, supportive, and united family. Through faith, open communication, and a commitment to growth, your family has embarked on a transformative journey.

Over the past **40 days**, you've taken important steps to create a strong foundation for your family's spiritual life. By nurturing your relationships, cultivating a supportive home environment, and fostering emotional and spiritual growth, you've given your family the building blocks for a life of love, unity, and faith.

The journey you've undertaken together is not only about the past **40 days** but also about the future you're creating for your family. Remember that building and maintaining strong family bonds is an ongoing process that requires patience, dedication, and love. As you continue to grow and evolve as a family, cherish the lessons you've learned and the experiences you've shared during this journey.

As you move forward, remain committed to nurturing the spiritual life of your family. Continue to pray together, study the Bible, and engage in meaningful conversations about faith. Embrace the power of family traditions and rituals, and strive to create a home environment that fosters love, understanding, and spiritual growth.

In the days, weeks, and years ahead, your family will inevitably encounter challenges and obstacles. Embrace these moments as opportunities to grow stronger and deepen your connection with one another. Remember the tools and strategies you've learned during this journey, and rely on your faith and the love of God to guide you through difficult times.

Finally, celebrate the beautiful, unique family that you are. Each member of your family brings their own gifts, talents, and perspectives, which enrich the whole. Treasure the journey you've shared and the memories you've created, and look forward to the future with excitement and anticipation.

As you conclude this **40-day journey**, remember that God is always with you, guiding and supporting your family in your quest for love and unity. May your family continue to grow in faith, love, and understanding, and may you always feel the presence of God's grace in your lives.

Heavenly Father, thank You for walking with us on this 40-day journey to strengthen our family bonds. We are grateful for the growth, understanding, and love that we've experienced along the way. Help us to continue building strong, lasting relationships, and guide us as we nurture our family's spiritual life.

In Jesus' name, Amen.

Thank you, Faith Shepherd

Faith Shepherd's books offer a powerful and inspiring message of hope, faith, and love. Her books are perfect for those seeking to deepen their spiritual journey and grow in their relationship with God.

Through her insightful and thought-provoking writing, **Faith Shepherd** shares practical wisdom and guidance for living a more purposeful and fulfilling life.

If you're looking for uplifting and inspiring reading material, don't hesitate to check out Faith Shepherd's books!

Copyright © Faith Shepherd, 2023

Made in the USA
Columbia, SC
07 December 2024

48634995R00067